Panorama-Books:

LAKE CONSTANCE

With thirty colour plates

KLAUS BRANTL

LAKE CONSTANCE

Introduction by

WILHELM VON SCHOLZ

Translated by Dorothy Plummer

MUNICH

WILHELM ANDERMANN VERLAG

Wrapper and cover designed by Gerhard M. Hotop

U.S. Distributors
FRENCH & EUROPEAN PUBLICATIONS Inc.
Rockefeller Center, New York, N. Y.

The Lake of Constance and its setting form a landscape of colour. — Not that any one colour predominates, as, for example, in lake Garda, where one can look down from the deck of a steamer into an indigo blue such as one seldom sees in other waters even from a distance above the shores. No, the shades of colour in the lake of Constance are of extreme diversity, and I know from many a painter along the lake that it has taken him years to master the palette required to render the multiplicity of light changes over the water, along the wooded shores, beneath the rocky hills, or the refraction of their counterpart in the lake. The morning or evening light, or still noon haze over the unruffled surface, present innumerable problems of rendition. The firmament alone which spans the "Swabian Sea" is a spectacle of infinite variety; the clouds, dazzling white or sombrely pregnant, move over the water in various combinations of the spectrum. The changing tints of green caused by the wind over the waves, now a breeze ruffling the surface, now a strong, blustering gale, or the hurricane heralding the storm and lashing the surface like a mighty organ fugue — offer constantly new aspects to the watchful eye.

Since my last years at school I have lived in my parents' house "Seeheim" by the lake, and even I am often amazed at the changes in the sky and the water. I can understand that it takes years for painters to become familiar with and to master all the magic effects of the atmosphere over the lake. This, then, is a reason which, in the case of the lake of Constance, justifies more than anywhere else the collection of coloured pictures to illustrate its beauty.

A further important aspect of the lake of Constance is that it is truly European. Around its shores, which present kindred natural features despite the greatest diversity of motif, five different states meet. Travelling from east to west, one passes from Austria to Bavaria, then to Wuerttemberg and Baden, now one state, across the Rhine in Constance, where the river discharges its waters into the lake, to the southern shore, eastwards again along the Swiss bank, which is also the longest, and back across the Rhine, where it flows inland again, to our Austrian starting point, Bregenz. West of Constance is the smaller and lower part of the lake, with a portion of the Rhine, and this, broadly speaking, is German in the north and Swiss in the south.

In the summer the population of these five states is increased by the affluence of countless tourists, and in the season the local inhabitants are scarcely to be found. The surroundings of the lake then become completely international. The roads are thronged with cars from every possible nation, and in the inns and on the lake's steamers the Anglo-Saxon and Latin tongues are heard equally.

The regular inhabitants, Swabians, Alemannic Germans, Austrians, Swiss, formed an entity, a living community, before the chaos of the two world wars. This sense of community has now begun to revive again. The hearts, thoughts, looks, and steps of these people were always dominated by the lake. Across its waters the towns and villages of one shore greet their neighbours on the other bank. The country around the lake forms a ring to a certain extent. In the course of the centuries the inhabitants came to develop a clan spirit, as it were, even though they may never have met. The cultural community they formed may almost be deemed a lake community, and this has remained indivisible in spite of erstwhile political force and territorial boundaries. All round the lake the population is German speaking, and in spite of the diversity reflected in art, literature and the tourist traffic, an unseen link welds it together, the unifying force of customs and habits.

The wanderer in these regions who climbs to some vantage point commanding a wide radius of view will see that the fair prospect offers contrasting possibilities. From the idyllic German hills and valleys he can ascend to the rocky snow summits which were reflected in the lake or which gleamed above the woods as he progressed along their paths. Down in the meadows of Swabia, by the shore near Friedrichshafen or Langenargen, he can find a resting-place in orchard green. In the wooded sandstone rocks of Bodman and Sipplingen he can work his way up through chill gorges to some venerable ruin overlooking the Ueberlingen bay and here, leaning back against the old wall, can gaze into the distance around the shores, which are as beautiful here as the shores of the lake of Geneva.

Down in the lower part of the lake there is a sanctuary for wild life and a variety of rare Alpine flora has been preserved. Here, when the evening glow lights up the Hegau, our wanderer will succumb to the enchantment of the plane. Light shreds of mist are wafted across his path, and the consistency of objects near and far dwindles to smoke. Near-by poplar trees, distant castles, churches, farms, are barely distinct above the level of water and land, — unreal, tenuous, as though the wind would bear them away.

Around the Reichenau and other sunny islands tall rushes surround the shores and conceal the breeding-places of swans, crested grebes and other water-fowl. Finally, further west, where the lower lake shrinks to a river again between high wooded banks, standing beneath the painted frescos of the old houses in Stein on Rhine, our traveller can see the current pulling away into distant lands, where it will develop into a mighty waterway.

Thus many days of wandering will be linked up and acquire cohesion. With the inward eye the wanderer will contemplate the wide landscape he has traversed, and the hazy background with its dim colours, and the high lights and shade immediately around him will gradually take shape and form a picture like an old German master, a vast canvas but animated with innumerable small, clearly sketched and colourful motifs. Towns and villages, castles on hillside or lake, look-out towers, harbours and churches, factory chimneys and gleaming railway tracks pattern the scene near and far, if only as dots or suggestive strokes. They give the landscape which they animate both human and cultural richness.

But we who live by the lake and are used to wander over or around it, whether by steamer, by motor-boat, behind a peaceful sail or with a pair of oars, whether by car, by bicycle or on foot, — we know that we are united by one common bond — our love for the lake, our devotion to the lake. And this from childhood's days! Small boys have always found a playground in the waves which curl on the shore. How lightly their flat pebbles skim and bound over the smooth water! When older, as young men, they will swim or sail on the lake, or climb the high mountains from whose summit they can view the silver bowl beneath them; as adults they will till the land, tend the vines and the orchards, our pride — near Meersburg and Hagnau, or on the island of Reichenau. They will serve the cause of art, of science or of industry — and then, one day, — how soon! — they will sit down by the shore again, hoary-headed, gazing into the glistening waves.

From the German side the view over the lake of Constance is dominated by the crenellated wall of the snow mountains rising behind the foothills on the southern shore. Beneath these mighty crags a glacier from the same primeval past has melted into a lake which mirrors the rocky heights. The Alpstein group, the Saentis, with its second summit, the Altmann — like a gigantic frog's head with two bulging eyes on the watch for water-flies —, to the east of the Saentis the Hohenkasten and Kamor, to the west the jagged peaks of the Churfirsten, are the giants which hold our gaze. But to the east of this massif still higher peaks soar up behind the ridge. The Scesaplana, Zimba, Rote Wand and Widderstein lure the mountaineer, and to the west of the Saentis the Glaernisch rears its head.

Down below these ramparts, almost seven hundred metres above sea-level, is the Swiss town of Sankt Gallen with the cathedral built by Bagnato and Thum, two masters of baroque art. Among the treasures of the magnificent collegiate library is the handwritten text of the Nibelungenlied and the parchment notice-book of St Gall in which he translated words of Swiss dialect into Latin. Before the Alps, in the Austrian Vorarlberg, is Dornbirn with its imposing Rappenlochschlucht, and Bregenz, where, from the Pfaendergebirge, one can see right over the lake to Constance on clear days.

This peaceful and scenically beautiful border territory was important in the earliest eras of history. After the long, prehistoric years of the glacial period, with the scanty half-life of dripping ice, splintering floes, and boulders that were carried away inch by inch in the waves; after equally long years as fen-country lost to the world, — a rainy, sombre area devoid of life and movement, save for a few solitary reptiles and occasional wild-fowl, — after these long, long years the first men arrived. Proof of these oldest human settlements was discovered in remains of the lake-dwellings they built.

In these far-off times the first lake inhabitants had to guard against both human enemies and wild animals. They erected their homes on a foundation of beams which they spread across piles driven into shallow water near the bank. The only means of access to these primitive habitations was from the lake, by canoe, that is to say, in the hollowed-out tree-trunks which served as canoes and which carried the lake-dwellers out into deeper waters to fish.

Each of the larger towns around the lake of Constance has a museum with remains from these early days. In Constance, in particular, the fine Rosgarten Museum, founded by the Leiner family, boasts a representative collection of objects illustrating the development of civilization around the lake.

But more graphic than all the museum exhibits of beams, arrow-heads and flint knives, are the life-size models of lake-dwellings which have been erected in the vicinity of Uhldingen, a small fishing village near Ueberlingen. These faithful reproductions of the earliest human habitations are fitted up as our ancestors knew them and can be visited by the passer-by.

The Romans penetrated to the Swabian Sea and for a short time to the Swabian land beyond. Their legions marched along the Roman highway, which stretched from Bregenz (Brigantium) through the Swiss Arbon (Arbor felix) and Constance (Constantia), — all frontier fortresses — in the middle is now Romanshorn, a harbour for the ferry service — and on through the small town of Coblenz (Confluentes) to Basel (Basilea). The present highway has been built along the old route.

The culture of the Mediterranean peoples then penetrated into our territory and numerous relics of architecture, jewellery and pottery have been discovered from these far-off times.

Politically the lake of Constance became important for the first time in the Middle Ages, in the days when the German emperors had no fixed residence but only the numerous palaces scattered over their domains in which they resided turn by turn. The imperial palace by the lake was Bodman Castle which gave its name to the lake, and gradually common usage slurred the name Bodmansee to Bodensee — lake of Constance.

Monasteries, which were in general the cradles of learning, were important also for the culture of the Swabian and Alemannian peoples. The prestige of the monastery in St. Gallen and of its fellow on the island of Reichenau was such that the latter became almost a seminary for the chancellors of the German Empire. Only the monks possessed the knowledge of language and script which was indispensable for such high office. The first lake-poetry, in Latin, was also born in the cloisters; the monks Walafried Strabo and Notker Balbulus composed sequences, solemn and light-hearted verse, and Eckehard wrote the Waltharilied.

But poetry blossomed more fully in the Hohenstauffen period (1138—1254), when it became the voice of chivalry. In the great castles all around the knights were the Minnesingers and sang their praise of the ideal in verse. The most important of these poets by the lake was probably Burkhard von Hohenfels (the ruins of his castle can be seen at Haldenhof, near Sipplingen), and a latecomer was the Minnesinger, Heinrich Suso, who subsequently became prior in the monastery of the Dominican order at Constance, now the Insel Hotel.

In 1183 at the Imperial Diet in Constance Friedrich Barbarossa made peace with the Lombard cities. But even greater fame accrued to the city through the ecclesiastical council held there between 1414 and 1418 at which the Bohemian religious reformer, John Huss, was sentenced to death at the stake, and the burgrave of Nuremberg was given the feudal estate of the March of Brandenburg. Glimpses of the profaner side of life at the grand synod have been handed down to us by Oswald von Wolkenstein, one of the latest Minnesingers. Banquets, song and dance are reflected in his verse, and stanzas in praise of fair women, as befitted the court poet of the times. Here and there we obtain a glimpse of social conditions, as, for example, when he scolds at the high price of eggs!

Constance was the centre of the German Empire in those days, that is to say, the hub of the world! For years it was the residence of the emperor and his government and of a motley pageant of princes, nobles, cardinals, bishops, abbots and priests. All categories of retainers as well as the usual jugglers and prostitutes increased the population. Both West and East sent their delegates to the Council. Chrysoloras, the delegate from Byzantium, died in the Dominican monastery during the synod, and his epitaph runs as follows:

"My ancestors are from Rome, I myself was born in Byzantium, the famous city of the East. My ashes rest in Constance. Where death strikes is of no moment. Everywhere on earth a like span separates us from heaven and from the place of eternal punishment."

One of the finest short stories of the great writer Conrad Ferdinand Meyer, who also celebrated in a poem to Huss the bishop's residence Gottlieben on the Rhine waters of the lake, takes place in Münsterlingen, in the Swiss canton of Thurgau, where Oswald von Wolkenstein danced. The story: "Plautus im Nonnenkloster" (Plautus in the Nunnery) breathes the spirit of the great Council of Constance. —

How a portion of the earth can suffer drastic changes at the hands of time is a feature of history which never fails to impress. Gone are the centuries when the lake shores resounded with exploits from centres of power, from autonomous princes' and bishops' seats, from citadels, Reich cities, like Constance and Ueberlingen, and centres of German trade, or monasteries, the home of culture. The centres of present-day activity have long since been transferred to a few big cities; the one great hub of past life has been relegated to the outskirts of human affairs, to the rank of a border town.

A few offshoots of the Thirty Years' War spread down to the lake; a Swedish flotilla sailed its waters and threatened the towns on its banks. The last shot of the great war of religion was fired in Lindau.

A small wave from the tide of Napoleonic events also broke on our shores. My home on the lake, near the Eichhorn, a former residence of the Order of the Teutonic Knights who had their headquarters at the castle on the island of Mainau, belonged at the beginning of the nineteenth century, together with the Arenenberg in Thurgau on the lower part of the lake, to Queen Hortense of Holland, the mother of Napoleon III. In the days of his youth the latter had many friends in Constance and the neighbouring Swiss resorts, and as a dancer was much in favour with the young ladies around the lake, before he started on his fateful dance with the goddess of history. Castle Arenenberg contains many souvenirs of the Bonapartes down to the unfortunate Prince Loulou who perished in Africa.

All historical greatness in this land belongs to the past. But life in general, the material from which history is built, the ground in which the passing centuries have left their mark, remains the same. Even in the solitude of the evening glow on a silent hill above the lake — perhaps on the Edelstein near Meersburg — nature pursues her eternal round: smoke arises from the hearth of cottage and mansion, a vehicle whisks along the road by the lake, fisher-boats are outlined on the gleaming water where a passing breeze darkens the surface and a distant steamer draws its furrow. In the vineyards late workers make their way down the slopes, and harvesters wend their way home; children at play, passing carts with baskets of fruit, evening bells lost in the dimness across the water — the pulse of nature beats incessantly.

And now across the gradually darkening lake! To the east, where a whisp of smoke betrays the passage of the steamer, the ruffled surface is merged in cool, gray-blue, lit up by the changing light of the moon. As we move westwards deep red illuminates the folds of the Hegau and the broad back of the Schienerberg on our left, in the south, above the high banks of the Rhine. The silhouette of a town is now visible in the evening glow, blotting out the more distant mountains, — a dark line between the fading sky and its broken reflection in the lake. The silhouette is animated by quivering lights which dance in the water. The great contours of the town — long lines of roofs pierced by smaller towers, the soaring spire of the cathedral — breaks up at our approach into massive, spacious groups of buildings, some to the fore, others retreating in the gloom. After a glance to our right, where the flat arches of the Rhine bridge span the gleaming river, we glide into the harbour of the old Reich city and bishop's residence, Constance.

The harbour is still alive, even at this late hour, as the last boats come and go. Fragments of music are wafted over from the public gardens by the lake and mingle with the throbbing of the steamer and the laughter and tumult on the lighted quay. A train moves into the near-by station. And above all the momentary activity by the water's edge soars the first symbol of the old city, the great gabled roof of the "Mart" — wrongly called the "Council Building". Once the waves broke against its foundations and the loaded freight boats landed right by the broad, Gothic door. Nowadays the floor of the lake has been filled and a big landing and unloading place has been built.

On penetrating into the town we wander through the nocturnal streets. The noise in the harbour has died down, not a soul is abroad, the moon, high in the sky, illuminates gables, oriels and sloping roofs, and casts a shimmer over the sleeping houses.

14

The night and the moon are master-builders. They build massively; the weight of their foundations can be felt; the edges of the soaring cubes are sharp. The stone is washed of its interplay of styles as if the latter were some tawdry finery imposed by men in the course of the centuries. Whole streets are now uniform and breathe the same great simplicity: soaring, sleeping stone!

Our footsteps ring on the irregular paving and an invisible, groping echo accompanies us in the distance.

We are in the city of the mighty, militant bishops, of patrician families and rebellious guilds; the city where the Emperor resided and held his diets and councils; the medieval Reich city which suffered the devastation of the plague, the slaughter of Jews, and famine, not to mention the all-destructive fires which leapt from roof to roof through the narrow streets and reduced whole quarters to dust and ashes.

We arrive at an old gate surmounted by a tower, with, next to it, a portion of the old city wall. Once it was closed at this nocturnal hour and a watchman was on guard in his look-out near the clock. It is the Schnetztor. Here the bishops rode into the city along the highway from Emmishofen in Switzerland.

A light gleams behind the coloured panes of an oriel window. Is it possible that the town clerk is still bent over his chronicles?

A high, gabled house stands out in the moonlight. The beam with the pulley and rope projects from under the roof and throws a sharp shadow on the narrow, shimmering house-wall. Here, in the days when "tela di Constanza" was world-famous, hundreds of bales of linen were drawn up into the gabled loft. —

Laughter and the ring of dice emerge from a tavern as we make our way towards the cathedral. Gradually it stands out from among the surrounding houses; only at the back, in the darkness of the trees, a smaller church and erstwhile monastery building lean up against what was once the church of the bishops of Constance.

Opposite, behind the stagnant waters of a small canal, other trees rustle in the darkness of the island, in the old Dominican monastery which Heinrich Suso once ruled as abbot, and which is now the Insel Hotel with its famous cloisters and historical frescos.

Again we enter dark, narrow streets leading down to the Rhine. Two towers stand out by the river; the one on the eastern side was formerly a gateway to a bridge, a planked way which led over the river into the town. Now, the gate is like a roofed, open gallery over the Rhine. We listen to the splashing of the waves, the swinging of heavy boats at their stakes; across the water the willows rustle in the night breeze; up the river before the open bay we see the sombre arches of the new bridge over which a brightly-lit train thunders into the city.

And silence enfolds the surroundings again. The city sinks back into sleep and the solitary step in the deserted streets resounds in its century-old dream.

The visitor can spend days visiting Constance with its fine Renaissance courtyard in the city hall, the magnificent baroque government building which was formerly the home of a cathedral canon, other more modest but equally fine architecture, and the beautiful natural surroundings. The town is the most important point on the western side of the lake. From Constance it is only a short distance on foot to Kreuzlingen on Swiss soil; to the monastery church with the fine carvings relating the history of the Passion; to the old bishop's castle in Gottlieben and the romantic "Drachenburg"; to castles Arenenberg and Salenstein; to Steckborn on the lower lake with its little turreted castle, and, further still, to Schaffhausen and the roar of the Rhine falls. On the

Konstanz,
Konzilsgebäude

Constance,
The "Council Building"

Constance,
La Maison du Concile

Konstanz, Rathaushof

Constance,
Courtyard of the City
Hall

Constance,
L'hôtel de ville

Kreuzlingen, Stiftskirche
Kreuzlingen,
The monastery church
Kreuzlingen,
L'église collégiale

Stein am Rhein

Gottlieben, Drachenburg

Bregenz, Spiel auf dem See
Bregenz, Festival on the lake
Bregenz, Représentation au bord du lac

St. Gallen, Dom

St. Gallen,
The Cathedral

St. Gall, La Cathédrale

Dornbirn, Rotes Haus

Dornbirn,
The "Red House"

Dornbirn,
La Maison Rouge

Lindau, Rathaus
Lindau, The City Hall
Lindau, L'hôtel de ville

Lindau, Diebsturm
Lindau,
The "Thieves' Tower"

Blick von Bad Schachen
auf Lindau
View from Bad Schachen
across to Lindau
Lindau
vu de Bad Schachen

Am Hafen von Lindau
The harbour of Lindau
Le port de Lindau

Langenargen,
Schloß Montfort

Langenargen,
Castle Montfort

Langenargen,
Le château de Montfort

Friedrichshafen, Hafenbahnhof
Friedrichshafen, The railway station in the harbour
Friedrichshafen, La gare portuaire

Friedrichshafen, Schloßkirche

Meersburg, Das Obertor

Meersburg,
The Upper Gate

Meersburg,
La porte du haut

Meersburg

Meersburg, Steiggasse
Meersburg,
In the old town
Meersburg,
Un vieux quartier

*In der Klosterkirche
von Birnau*
Interior of the monastery
church of Birnau
Dans l'église de Birnau

Birnau, Baumblüte
Birnau,
Blossoming fruit trees
Le printemps à Birnau

Sipplingen

Mittelzell
auf der Insel Reichenau

Mittelzell
on the island of Reichenau

L'île de Reichenau,
Mittelzell

Auf der Insel Mainau
On the island of Mainau
L'île de Mainau

Hohentwiel

Radolfzell, Ölberg

German bank the western road leads to Radolfzell and the Hohentwiel, places reminiscent of Scheffel.

On the eastern side, travelling from Constance to the upper shores and to the arm of the lake by Ueberlingen, the visitor can cross the car-ferry to Meersburg and visit the famous old castle from Merovingian times. He will be drawn also to the places which commemorate the great Westphalian poetess, Annette von Droste-Hülshoff, Mesmer, the Austrian physician and author of mesmerism, and Fritz Mauthner, the famous philologist. Further to the west along the shore is the monastery of Birnau. Its baroque church and panorama from the site on the hill never fail to attract pilgrims and tourists. Only the fine apartments of the abbot in the monastery can no longer be visited now that the Cistercian monks have returned.

Opposite Birnau is the island of Mainau, formerly the residence of the grandduke and duchess of Baden, now the heritage of their Swedish kinsfolk: an isle of bliss which recalls the Isola Bella in Lago Maggiore and which displays southern, even tropical plant-life and enchants the tourist with its flowers. In the hothouses there are real coffee shrubs since the days after the war when Heinz Grosse, a former plantation owner, planted seeds he had brought from Africa on German soil, and the experiment proved a success.

A centre of attraction in the north-west is Ueberlingen, the second former Reich city on the lake. The late Gothic cathedral contains a magnificently carved high altar-piece by Jörg Zürn; the birth-place of Suso can be visited

Konstanz, Münster und Rheintorturm
Constance, The Cathedral and tower of the Rhine Gate
Constance, La cathédrale et la tour du Rhin

in the town, and in the park one can walk on the site of the old moats beneath the city wall; the museum, in the former patrician mansion of the Reichlin-Meldegg, is also of interest. In the hinterland is the so-called Linzgau and the former monastery of Salem, now the seat of the margraves of Baden, with the well-known boarding school of the same name; a little further away, on the hill, stands the princely residence Heiligenberg, and not far removed is the Haldenhof with its all-embracing view. Opposite, a few minutes by motor-boat, is the village of Bodman, with Bodman Castle in its well-tended park, behind it the contours of the Frauenberg; further up, on the wooded slopes, is the romantic Marienschlucht and above the gorge the castle ruins of Kargegg.

The focal points on the eastern side of the lake are the towns of Bregenz and Lindau which lie in a certain proximity to each other beneath the picturesque foot-hills of the high Austrian and Swiss mountains.

Bregenz is the starting point for tours in the Pfaender group and the gateway to the Vorarlberg and the principality of Liechtenstein. In recent years Bregenz has become famous for its theatre, both through the summer performances on the lake and through the visits from the Vienna Burgtheater which attract strangers from near and far.

Lindau itself is an interesting city with fine examples of old architecture: the so-called "Pagan Wall" dating from Roman times, a town-hall in the Renaissance style, the turreted "Thieves' Tower" the old arcades with street vendors in the high street, the former stately baroque residence of Freiherr von Seutter which now houses a museum — nearby the much-visited Bad Schachen and the idyllic little peninsula Wasserburg.

Between Lindau and Meersburg, past Castle Montfort, we find Friedrichs-hafen. Connected by a car-ferry with Romanshorn on the opposite Swiss bank it is mainly a centre of attraction for the visitor with technical interests. Here Count Ferdinand Zeppelin designed and built his airships, which once filled the whole world with amazement and connected the small town on the lake of Constance in regular flights with Lakehurst in USA. But the technical history of Friedrichshafen is actually much older: at the beginning of the nine-teenth century it saw the launching of the first lake steamer, christened "Wil-helm" after the king of Wuerttemberg. The city has kept its technical character and renown but possesses equally important cultural features in the former royal castle and erstwhile monastery church Hofen in the castle park.

Apart from the living population around the lake of Constance there is a still race of beings to be found on its shores, symbolic of a venerable civili-zation. Like us they express pain, desire, contemplation, agitation, hatred and love. But, since they are silent, immobile, immutable, their existence is for all time, whereas we, the loudly gesticulating, pass on.

These still figures, secular or profane, are the works of art, the men and women in cathedrals and churches, on old city buildings or patrician houses, in the homes of the townspeople and in museums!

By lingering in their company one gains friends to be visited again and again. In contemplation before such aspects of life, held fast by the hand of art, one realizes more and more that the fundamentals of human existence have never changed. These figures tell us that what is important and essential was the same hundreds of years ago, a clearly described circle of duties, happiness and pain, work and festivities, service and care.

If one sinks into an empty pew before the famous wood-carving of the

"Annunciation" in the little church down in the lower part of Meersburg, one's perception of the simple fervour and absorption expressed in the sculpture gradually gives way to an awareness of the miracle which is taking place.

In the Heiligenberg chapel the Madonna with her halfclosed eyelids breathes majesty and stillness before the eternal, immutable laws of existence. These laws, like the round of life in general, are reflected in all the figures which have been hallowed by art and yet given a worldly form, as, for example, the family, the shepherds and the animals of Jörg Zürn's high altar in the cathedral at Ueberlingen. The longer we remain in contemplation of these sculptures the greater their power of attraction.

But not only for those who seek religious solace are such works of art a reality. Others are riveted by the life imprisoned by the artist in stone. For the art historian they unveil history. But in order to enjoy them no such specialized knowledge is needed — merely a feeling for the crystal-clear humanity rendered by the artist's hand. Above all, one must feel a certain love for this Swabian-Alemannic race with its austere fervour and artistic perception of the eternal in human life.

TO THE PICTURES

Constance, The "Mart"

The "Mart" which is wrongly known as the "Council Building", was built towards the end of the 14th century by an architect whose name has been handed down as "Master Arnold". He fell in the so-called Appenzeller War, probably in 1404 in the Battle of Speicher. The building served as a storehouse where the big sailing vessels unloaded their cargoes of corn or wine. In early times also the big linen fairs were held there and "tela di Constanza", which was famous in the Middle Ages, was bartered by dealers from near and far. For a long time the building stood right by the water; the terraces in front of it now were built up at a later date.

The erroneous name "Council Building" derives from the fact that, whereas the main sessions of the Council of Constance were held in the Cathedral, the large, upper room of the "Mart" was used for the Conclave at which in 1417 the Roman, Otto von Colonna, was elected pope and became Martin V, thus putting an end, at least formally, to the schism which had divided Christianity into three factions under three mutually hostile popes.

Just as in those days the great rooms of the "Mart" were used for meetings, the two large halls of the building are now used for concerts, exhibitions and gatherings of all kinds.

Constance, Courtyard of the City Hall

The original city hall was down by the fish market. At the beginning of the 18th century it was replaced by a new building destined to hold various offices of the municipal administration. The main door, which was taken from the earlier edifice, conveys but a slight impression of its architectural beauty.

Between 1593 and 1600 alterations were made in the house of the Mercers' Guild, which now became the present city hall. Its façade, with frescos from a later period, stretches along the Kanzleistraße. As it now stands, the city hall is one of the finest buildings in the town. The picture shows the Renaissance courtyard, with fine sculptures on the façade of the rear wing. For years this beautiful setting, which has the atmosphere of a pallace, was used for performances in the open air.

Kreuzlingen

The monastery attached to the church in our picture was originally an abbey belonging to a religious community of knights, but all the records relating to its foundation were lost by fire and pillage in the frequent wars. It is uncertain, therefore, whether, as tradition maintains, the monastery was actually founded in the 10th century by Conrad the Venerable, bishop of Constance, or whether it was not founded until the beginning of the 12th century by another bishop of Constance, Ulrich von Kyburg. In any case, the church and adjacent monastery, as they stand today, were rebuilt in the 17th century after frequent destruction in earlier times and later fires. The buildings now serve as a seminary. The wonderful carvings of the Passion in the church are famous. Some thousand figures, delicately chiselled in wood, people the vast hilly background.

Stein on Rhine

The little Swiss town of Stein nestles between sloping vineyards crowned by the proud castle of Hohenklingen (once the seat of the von Klingenberg family), and the Rhine. At this point the river has scarcely left the lower arm of the lake and a graceful old bridge joins the northern bank — the first crossing point after the Rhine bridge in Constance — with the southern bank.

The market place in Stein is always a centre of attraction. The picturesque facades of the famous old houses which surround it, with their gaily painted frescos, carry one far back into the

Middle Ages, as though time had stood still.

Even more important in our picture is the monastery of St George with its foundations washed by the Rhine. Apart from the charm of its location the fine Renaissance building is also remarkably well preserved. Visitors will make their way past the austere monastic cells to impressive halls (approximately 1515) in which the gaily painted walls are spanned in some cases by vaulted wooden ceilings. The monastery was restored and kept up in an exemplary manner by the former owner, Ferdinand Vetter. Today it belongs to the state.

Steckborn

This small town is situated on the lower arm of the lake on the picturesque road from Kreuzlingen to Schaffhausen. The old castle in the town, now called the "tower", was built in 1342 by Abbot Diethelm from the Reichenau against rebel monks.

In the course of its history it was used in turn as a place for barter and for storage, as an alms-house and a museum.

Travellers going down the river to Schaffhausen are fascinated by the four towers of the medieval stronghold, now a public monument.

Gottlieben — Drachenburg

Gottlieben is a small Swiss village on the Rhine near Constance opposite the German Wollmatinger Ried (a wild-life reserve with Alpine flora which were originally carried down in the glacial epoch, thousands of years ago). Gottlieben ist a favourite place for excursions on account of its picturesque old inns. The so-called Drachenburg and the Waaghaus are still run in the old Swiss style.

Near-by stands the former bishop's castle where the religious reformer, John Huss, was imprisoned in one of the towers under the roof. The castle, with its thickly grown park, once belonged to Emperor Napoleon III, who had Gothic windows from a broken-off portion of the cathedral cloisters in Constance built into the frontage of his castle along the Rhine. Later the von Fabrice family lived there and today it is the home of the well-known singer, Lisa della Casa.

Romanshorn

Romanshorn, probably named after a certain "Romanus", who colonized one of the points in the big Swiss bay between Arbon and Romanshorn, was a village which has now become a modern traffic centre. With its two churches standing above the lake and charming cluster of houses on the hilly shore it is important as the terminus of the ferry from Friedrichshafen and for railway connexions with Bregenz and Constance, or Zurich and St Gallen.

Bregenz

Bregenz is the Austrian harbour (Vorarlberg) on the lake beneath the Pfaendergebirge. The latter ridge is famous for the view it offers across the lake to Constance. An aerial railway leads up to the summit. About halfway up the slope is the little chapel of St Gebhard from where one looks down onto the upper part of the town with its picturesque fortifications and stately gateway.

Between the Pfaender and the lake is a narrow defile, the "Bregenzer Klause", which was the scene of violent combats in the Thirty Years' War. Led by field marshal Wrangel the Swedes succeeded in taking the gorge and then conquered the city, which suffered great damage and hardship.

In summer Bregenz now has the most popular open-air theatre around the lake and is a starting point for a variety of excursions and mountain tours in the beautiful Bregenzerwald.

St. Gallen

The town of St. Gallen, capital of the canton, grew up around the monastery founded by St Gall in the 7th century. The town is one of the highest in Europe. It possesses a famous library with many works of great value, including costly manuscripts such as a psalter of Notker Labeo from the 10th century and an important manuscript of the Lay of the Nibelungs from the 13th century. St Gallen is also the city of the reformer Vadian, a disciple of Zwingli. An impressive monument commemorates his name.

Climbing tours in the Alpstein mountains, to the Saentis, Altman and Hohenkasten all start from St. Gallen (via Gais and Appenzell). The town is a big industrial centre and has become world-famous for its embroidery.

Dornbirn, The "Red House"

The small country town in the Vorarlberg, with architectural treasures like the "Red House" is known above all for the romantic gorge in the vicinity — the "Rappenloch-Schlucht".

Lindau and Bad Schachen

The last shot of the Thirty Years' War was fired in Lindau. The city was also the birth-place of the poet Hermann Lingg, and witnessed the brief connubial bliss of Emanuel Geibel, who sang the praise of Lindau in his verse. — The architecture of the town, which is well-preserved, dates from various periods and goes back to Roman times, the so-called "Pagan Wall" being a relic of these early days. The city hall, an attractive Renaissance building, was restored in the 19th century by Thiersch. Old-fashioned arcades line the high-street and give shelter to street vendors selling their wares. On the market square is the regional museum in a stately old patrician house (once the residence of Freiherr von Seutter). The "Thieves' Tower", a former prison, is a round structure, capped by a gracefully pointed tower flanked by turrets.

The finest view of the island city of Lindau is from the neighbouring resort, Bad Schachen. Here visitors can enjoy the up-to-date beach and magnificent adjoining park of the Lindenhof, whose wall runs along the shore.

The harbour of Lindau with its busy shipping traffic against the background of the high Austrian and Swiss mountains is one of the most impressive sights around the lake of Constance. The entrance to the harbour is guarded on the one side by a lion carved in Kelheim marble by the sculptor Halbig, and on the other side by a lighthouse. The Bavarian lion on its high granite pedestal at the end of the eastern jetty is a landmark for tourists arriving from the lake. Behind the harbour is a monument, also by Halbig, to Max II of Bavaria, under whose auspices the Munich—Lindau railway line was built. It is now one of the main approaches to the lake.

Wasserburg

This picturesque little peninsula with its castle-like edifice and church offers a magnificent view across the upper part of the lake to the Pfaender, Allgäu, Vorarlberg and Swiss mountains; opposite one can see the massif of the Saentis. Wasserburg was once the residence of Freiherr von Gleichen-Russwurm, a great-grandchild of Friedrich von Schiller.

Castle Montfort in Langenargen

The castle, a barracks-like building extending into the lake, was once the residence of a Princess Luise of Prussia. Its name recalls a prominent Vorarlberg family of nobility, to which the well-known Minnesinger, Hugo von Montfort, belonged.

Langenargen is a popular holiday resort.

Friedrichshafen

King Friedrich of Wuerttemberg laid out the harbour and a part of the town of Friedrichshafen in order to promote trade with Switzerland and Italy. The former monastery Hofen became the royal castle in the midst of a magnificent park. The old church belonging to the monastery is a favourite haunt of tourists on account of the famous and elaborate stucco-work in its interior. The two onion-shaped towers of the castle church, as it is now called, can be seen on a clear day across the lake.

Friedrichshafen is the terminus of the railway line from Ulm to the lake of Constance, and the port of embarkation for the ferry to Romanshorn. Between these two towns is the deepest point in the lake and also its greatest breadth.

The town was rebuilt after the destruction of the last war. The railway station in the harbour is an impressive example of modern architecture. A regular train service from this station links up the ferry with the main lines a short distance away.

The name of Graf Ferdinand von Zeppelin, the great airship pioneer, is irrevocably bound up with the history of Friedrichshafen, which even boasts a Zeppelin museum.

The first steamer to cross the lake of Constance, the royal paddle — steamer "Wilhelm", started from Friedrichshafen, and marked the beginning of a rapidly growing boat-service which only in recent times has been outdone by motor traffic.

Meersburg

Meersburg is by far the most picturesque little town on the lake. Its old castle, dating from Merovingian days, is said to have had its foundations laid by Charles Martel. The rock on which it stands was laid bare by serfs. In the nineteenth century the old castle belonged to the great German scholar Joseph Freiherr von Lassberg, who was responsible for saving the interesting old edifice when there was a danger that it might be pulled down. Lassberg's second wife often received visits from her sister, the famous poetess, Annette von Droste-Hülshoff, who composed the most beautiful poems that have ever been written in honour of the lake. The rooms in which she lived are open to the public, and also the death-chamber where she passed away on May 24, 1848. Between the old castle and the modern structure is a deep moat containing a mighty mill-wheel which has been preserved from olden times. A high bridge connects the two buildings. A double flight of steps, closed at the bottom by a remarkably beautiful wrought-iron gate, leads up to the wide terrace which dominates the lake. From here the visitor can enjoy a magnificent view around its shores. The new castle was built by Bagnato, in the baroque style, as a bishop's residence, and has an especially attractive hall. At a later date it became a home for the deaf and dumb. Nowadays it is a public monument.

Other large buildings originally intended for prelates but subsequently used for profane purposes stand next to the new castle. The one farthest to the east, with its fine courtyard, was formerly a seminary. The façades, to the right of the picture, form an unbroken line on the crest of the hill above the lake.

Steep alleys and flights of steps connect the lower town on the harbour — places of interest are the imposing Grethaus and the little church with its famous "Annunciation" — with the upper town. The different levels and angles from which one can regard the town offer a multitude of romantic views. Particularly charming is the view of the "Bären", an old inn with oriel, and behind it the tower of the upper gate, also the famous Steiggasse. Seen from the lake, in its setting of well-kept vineyards, Meersburg gives the impression of a little Italian hill-town.

Birnau

A monastery in the late baroque style with a church which is a well-known place of pilgrimage, Birnau was secularized for a time but now houses an order of monks again. For this reason the fine apartments belonging to the prior can no longer be visited. The interior of the church is spacious and elaborately decorated with innumerable cherubs and other fanciful ornamentation. Birnau stands on the hill above the lake near Ueberlingen.

Uerberlingen

Originally an old Alemannian settlement, called Iburningae or Iburinge, and now the hub of life on this arm of the lake, the town of Ueberlingen had the status of a free Reich city and with its old-world houses and nooks and winding lanes displays to a certain extent a medieval character. Visitors are attracted to the lofty late-Gothic cathedral chiefly on account of the famous wood-carvings by Jörg Zürn on the high altar. The composition of the numerous groups as well as of the individual figures is striking. In the town hall the tourist should visit a room with a finely carved wooden ceiling.

Up on the hill stands the former home of the Reichlin-Meldegg family, a fine patrician house which has now been converted into a museum. From its terrace one looks down onto the cathedral and the town, and across the narrow arm of the lake to the dark wooded crests of Bodman.

The mystic Heinrich Seuse (Suso) was born in Ueberlingen; a room reminiscent of him can be visited in the house of his birth. The most important event in the history of the town was probably the victory won by the citizens of Ueberlingen in the Thirty Years' War when they successfully repelled the Swedes under General Horn (1634).

The old towers and moats belonging to the fortifications have been preserved and fine parks have been laid out between them. An impressive cactus garden will delight the plant-lover.

On the road along the shore of the lake to Sipplingen one can visit the caves in the sandstone rocks which are familiar from Scheffel's "Eckehard".

In recent years Ueberlingen has become a spa visited for Kneipp treatment.

Sipplingen

An idyllic little resort, almost at the end of the Ueberlingen arm of the lake, Sipplingen ist enchanting when its fruit trees blossom in spring. In recent times a large pump station has been installed to supply drinking water to the hinterland as far as Stuttgart. Halfway up the hillside is the old castle Hohenfels, belonging to the Minnesinger Burkard. Farther on is the "Haldenhof", a popular place for excursions on account of the wide view, and with a "Minnesinger room" in memory of Burkard von Hohenfels.

Island of Reichenau

The first settlers on the island were brought by the Irish or Scottish monk Pirmin, and Reichenau became famous for its Benedictine abbey. In the Middle Ages the monastery was almost a seminary for the chancellors of the Reich who acquired there the learning which they needed for their high office. Well-known monks of the abbey were the poets Notker and Walahfrid Strabo, who wrote sequences and poems celebrating the island and its gardens. Three interesting churches dating back, in part, to the early Middle Ages, are famous for the relics they contain. Mittelzell, the largest of them, boasts relics of St Mark — which are coveted by the sister church, San Marco, in Venice — and a drop of the Sacred Blood which is carried every year in a special procession. The tomb of Charles the Fat can also be visited there. The sacristy of the church still harbours objects which are described by Viktor von Scheffel in "Eckehard", as, for example, the big, coloured enamel, and also a pitcher supposed to have been used at the Marriage in Cana for the conversion of water to wine. The oldest church on the island is the church of St George in Oberzell, where the skull of this saint is preserved. St George's is probably the most classical example of early church architecture in the whole of the region around the lake.

The sunny, unwooded island is famous today for the vegetables grown in its market gardens.

Mainau

Formerly the seat of the Order of the Teutonic Knights, then owned by Count Douglas, the island became the summer residence of the grandduke and duchess of Baden, and was visited occasionally by Emperor Wilhelm I, the father of the grandduchess Luise. Now Mainau is the property of the Swedish Count Bernadotte, who has devoted himself to the culture of the southern and partly tropical flora, and has turned the island into a great centre of attraction for strangers. Apart from its summer visitors Castle Mainau has an independent existence as the headquarters of the International Institute founded by Count Bernadotte as an amalgamation of the world famous Young Men's Christian Association movements and of the World League of these movements.

Hohentwiel

Standing on a volcanic hill in the Hegau near the growing industrial town of Singen, the Hohentwiel, compared with other castle ruins in the Hegau, is manifestly an old fortress. As such it played an important part in the Thirty Years' War. The brave commander of the fort, Conrad Wiederholt, is still remembered today for his successful defense of the stronghold in the name of his master, the duke of Wuerttemberg. Hohentwiel has remained a portion of Wuerttemberg enclosed in Baden, although these two states are now one. It is famous as the background of the greater part of Viktor von Scheffel's novel "Eckehard". From its ruined walls there is a fine view across the hill-tops of the Hegau to the distant chains of mountains.

Radolfzell

The most important place on the lower part of the lake. The so-called "little Austrian castle", crowned with turrets, is well worth visiting.

In the customary floodlighting of historical buildings the old tower of the Rhine gate, which once gave onto a wooden bridge connecting Constance with the barbican Petershausen, offers the most picturesque impression of the town at the point where lake and river converge. In the background is the cathedral tower with the nineteenth century perforated spire.

PANORAMA-BOOKS

Germany: BAVARIA · BAVARIAN ROYAL CASTLES · BERLIN
THE BLACK FOREST · HAMBURG · MUNICH · LAKE CONSTANCE
THE RHINE · ROMANTIC GERMANY · THE RUHR

Austria: CARINTHIA · SALZBURG AND SURROUNDINGS
TYROL · VIENNA

France: ALSACE · CHATEAUX OF THE LOIRE · CÔTE D'AZUR
FRENCH CATHEDRALS · PARIS · PROVENCE

Italy: CAPRI · FLORENCE · THE GULF OF NAPLES
ROME · SICILY · VENICE

Scandinavia: COPENHAGEN · FINLAND · LAND OF THE
MIDNIGHT SUN · NORWAY · SWEDEN

Capitals of the world: ISTANBUL · LONDON · MOSCOW · PEKING
NEW YORK

Other countries: BALEARIC ISLANDS · BERMUDA · GREECE
THE HOLY LAND · ISRAEL · LAKE GENEVA* · PORTUGAL
THE NETHERLANDS · SPAIN · SWITZERLAND
YUGOSLAVIA – Dalmatian Coast

* *In preparation*

EDITOR HANS ANDERMANN